The Prayer
Whisperer

The Prayer Whisperer

Poems and Prayers of Abandonment to Divine Love

James Kok

Prayer

Prayer is the wheat field of the soul's longing swaying in the breeze of truth. It is the fresh cut flowers of devotion reverently placed on the altar of God's love, as a yearning heart kneels at the feet of Omnipresence.

Through an offering of all-surrendering love for God the body and the mind recede and God becomes you.

Your prayer is God's and you are free.

Every prayer is relevant, a relevance that passes all understanding as it is whispered through eternity.

the author

Contents

Love's consent

Winding path of straw lit grace
Leading me ever closer to holy embrace
Yearning river, high rocks cascading heart
Night cries plagued by dreams painted art

Restless soul seeking truths unknown
Mind tortured habits keeping me alone
Delusions door remains wide open
Things seem real yet all is broken

Searching satisfaction's dark temptation
Pleasure imploring sense gratification
Crashing hopes lie in bits unattended
Holiness stalks, doubts apprehended

Moonlit joy's shining lake of stillness
Quiet mind resting on beams of realness
Awakened heart rising in wonder
What truth lies ahead for soul's plunder

Acid doubts corrode scenes of beauty
Senses attention claiming breached duty
Questions fly on rapids white water
Will's drowning cries splutter in slaughter

Frantic breaths grabbing life's force
Saving prayers uttered to their source
Gentle assurance, omnipresent mind
Clear holy light shines grace outlined

Love's shadows move across heart's face
Soul leaps in joy recognizing this place
Stars look like home but reaching higher
Omniscient steps tread on horizon's fire

Kindness reigns unattended fields of glory
Craggy peaks whisper truth's story
Devotion's blossoms lay at Thy feet
Born in heart's garden hidden and discreet

All are Yours that I have come to know
Humble sacrifice offered without show
Heart afire, joy's reaching hand
Wisdom tasted, Love's consent—O, Holy Land.

Divine Light of Spirit, reflecting on the river of my soul as it wanders towards Thee.

Warm wind of Love, blowing through the tall cedars of my heart ever whispering, "hold fast, hold fast and victory will be yours".

O the thrill, the joy of such words. I surrender again and again to Thee, seventy times seven.

Clouds of doubt evaporate, I am the sky. All worlds revolve within me. The river has become the Light. Omnipresence has become me.

Thank you, Lord, thank you.

My heart rejoices that You are every moment of my life. My soul smiles that not a syllable will be lost in our eternal discourse.

Each whisper will be heard and every loving gesture acknowledged. Nothing is lost in this place of constant gain.

As the sun caresses the breeze, so my heart kneels in surrender to You. The only want I have is You.

Upon waking I love You, in each moment my love seeks You. I am trapped by the kindness of Your invitation in wanting me.

O, Divine Lord, there are no more words, only You—God, God, God.

Divine Lord, do I give You first place in my heart? Do I turn only to You without a glance at my own self-reliance?

Do I count on You alone or am I holding some portion of myself from You?

O, Beloved One, immerse me in Yourself so that nothing exists outside of You.

Let no beat of my heart be for any other. Let no flash of delusion entice me from Your loving altar.

My prayer is that I will always see the poverty of my own self while offering everything I have as a sacrifice to You.

My being is filled with gladness, Faith has become me. Every footstep echoes Thy presence and my heart rests in Thee.

When thunder rolls and lightning flashes I fear no evil, for my heart rests in Thee.

It is my prayer, Blessed One, that I shall always feel Thee close and may every uttered word be filled with Truth.

The world stands firm, but through Thy grace, I have escaped its grip because my heart rests in Thee.

The river that flows through my heart—the sparkle of joy, its bubbling vitality, is that You?

How is it that You come in stillness, in the hush of first light and steal into my consciousness?

I surrender to You.

A gentle breeze of peace settles upon me and I rest as a prisoner of Love being led to You.

Victory is mine as You become me.

Holy Lord, do You love me when I have no thought of loving You?

Does Your joy surround me when I feel no joy within? Is Your peace with me when I show no peace to my neighbour?

Beloved God, help me that I may imitate You—dissolving into Your oneness.

Capture me that I may surrender to You.

O, Lord, I begin again each day, I begin as if I had never begun.

It is only the continuity of Love that bridges the gap of my forgetfulness. It is only Grace that flames the yearning of my heart.

Leave me not, Beloved One, lest I find myself in the desert of despair. Lest blinding darkness engulfs me.

Thou art the polestar of my life—shine brightly that I may never lose sight of Thee.

Beloved Lord, my eyes are set on Holiness, my heart is aflame with Love. When shall I capture Thee?

Is my trap not well set? Is my net not cast beyond the rocks of my indifference?

Come closer, Beloved One, as I bait the hooks of my joy with devotion.

Thou art the Harvest. I wait in anticipation of Thy grace, warmed by the everlasting light of Omnipresence.

I float on the waves of the Ocean, waiting to become It.

Divine Lord, I know that I am loved for it is Love that courses through my veins.

When I bleed, it is Love that comes forth. When I breathe, it is Love that flows in and out.

This Love gave me my birth and will sustain me in death. Each moment I receive It.

Help me to give Love as freely as it has been received— this is my prayer.

Help me, Beloved One, not to hold Love fast but to use it as the currency of my life, exchanging it for any bitterness and indifference that crosses my path.

May I be Love's banker, giving all I have to the poverty of those who have not.

Holy One, Thou art the summer of my heart. Love wafting above fields of green. Peace at rest in the warmth all around.

As streams of joy trickle over the toes of my soul, smiling I forget all form to wander between clouds of bliss and the high craggy peaks of devotion.

O, Beloved One, is the prisoner finally free? Has the cage of all desires been destroyed?

I know this to be so, for now, I see only Thee and my soul cries out as it reclaims its divine inheritance.

Thou who has always been, are mine and I am Thine.

Holy Lord, as my eyes turn towards the horizon of my hope, how far can I go?

Can I ask You to speak to me? Can I wander in the garden of Your love picking the fruit of indescribable joy?

What is the distance between You and me if we are One? What keeps us apart if there is only Love?

Beloved One, my life is limited only by the extent of my love. Make this love unconditional that all barriers might be transcended and the infinity of each moment made manifest.

Divine Lord, everything is so simple with You. The gentle breeze of kindness rests on every leaf as I walk in its midst.

Easy is Your love that smiles with every drop of rain, softly playing its melody of generosity as I listen to each note with joy.

My soul relaxes on the sunny porch of Your heart and adores You.

Thank you, Beloved One, all I want is You—how could I ask for anything more? How could I look for anything greater?

I surrender to You.

Lord, how can I love more? What depths can the heart plumb before love's full extent is reached?

Thou didst whisper that a greater love can only come from living to please Thee more—speaking with Thee and seeing Thy face in every place.

O, Love of all loves, how this thrills my soul. How it rejoices in the very thought of Thee.

Beloved One, turn my eyes upward and still this arrogant mind to serve Thee in every way.

Let not the simplicity of each moment escape Love's blush. Let not a thought go forth that is not of Thee.

O, heart's Saviour, I lay the flowers of my devotion before Thee. Hear my prayer. Accept me as a fertile garden where Thou canst freely plant the seeds of Thy love.

Divine Lord, what are these thoughts that wander through my mind?

Do I exist so that they might be, or are these wild horses meant to serve me?

How can I hope to be free with unruly friends who take up all of my time?

Truly are they not my enemies who need to be vanquished and ruled with an iron fist?

Strengthen me, Beloved One, to recognize these anarchists. Help me to still their protests—not one sound from these rebels can assist me.

It is Thy word alone I wish to hear. It is only Thy love I wish to feel.

Holy Lord, how sweet is our love. The tenderness of Your watchful glance assures me that all I want is You.

Drawing closer, the warmth of Your joy envelopes me in a peace without words.

My life is complete with the meaning that Your presence brings. My thoughts in You have satisfied my soul.

May I live in You with all the yearning of one who has been separated from his love.

May I always be with You even when I feel lost in the darkness of night.

O, my Love, accept me that I may know You, just You, my God.

Divine Lord, have I woven Thy love into the tapestry of my life? Do its threads knit into the most remote recesses of who I am?

Does kindness colour my fabric ensuring its visibility to all those around me?

Does joy spring forth from my soul giving to all those in need of drink? Does its moisture wet thirsty lips giving a taste of Thee?

I pray, Beloved One, that I increasingly do Thy will and that this is always done in Thee.

O, Divine Lord, who tells me that You are God?

Is it the heroes performing their indiscriminate acts of kindness? Or is it the humble who stand resolute before the wrath of the world?

Do the mountains that touch the sky not point to You or the ocean that laps its shores?

When the wheat fields sway with their harvest in the breeze of love or the wildflowers blossom, are they not calling out Your name?

O, Beloved One, forgive me when I do not recognize You, forgive my eye when it looks mundanely upon the presence of Your perfection.

In the womb of my heart, my soul knows You and it is waiting to come forth, O God, my saviour.

Am I alone with You my Lord? Is the secret of our love something that flows only between us?

Are my whispers of delight expressed in silent recognition of our bond, only heard by You?

Are the moments of Your response encouraging me to go deeper, come closer, just for me?

Beloved One, I am in You, immersed in the magnificence of Your love. A love that takes in sea and sky, I am lost therein without a trace.

All there is, is You, You, You. Can this bliss be heaven? Or is it just our secret when we are alone?

God of all things, every new leaf of spring points to Your Majesty. Every blossoming flower attests to Your glory.

Not a step can be taken without seeing the reflection of Your omnipresence in the sky.

O, Beloved One, You have cleared my sight to see within and without and now my soul rests in the cradle of Your joy.

I pray, O Glorious God, that You will strengthen and nurture me so that all is not lost when the days of winter dawn.

Holy Lord, how completely can I be with You? Can I be so close that Your tenderness becomes me—that its everlasting nature becomes mine?

Can You and I be eternal, without separation or division? Can breathlessness be shared? Can silent Truth be imparted?

O, Beloved One, what am I to do, how am I to be? Am I ready to accept You? Have I done enough or was there always nothing to do?

Lead me, Divine Love, the world is at my back and the path ahead shines brightly. My soul is restless in love and listens only for Your silent whisper.

O, the peace of not another thought, not another desire— just You, You, You, my God.

Enemies best friends

Whispered word crossing plains of creation
Primeval birds, eyes down in lose formation
Life streams licking scorched property
Spotted hyenas laughing in mockery

Conditioned mind searching satisfaction's effect
Vultures picking brain's last respect
Media offering truth for a penny
Where do I stand, with one or with many

Morals waver, conscience burns
Subjects bow without concerns
Dictator reigns this land of right
Sight gone black shining bright night

Hunger craving illusive something
Cold days hell where meanings trusting
Can redemption's will save me still
Intuitive soul's doing a fire drill

Love birthing through grace's labour
Hijacked thoughts seek unshackled favour
Soul's stirring cry beneath life's debris
Am I more than I seem to be

Head beating throbs floating neon sea
Innocent madness, narcissistic sanity
Spirit searching waters ever-living well
Bartering desires ring liberty's bell

Soul stands resolute battling imposters undaunted
Fight to the death each throat cut and quartered
Enemies best friends, frauds family
Victory denied, wounded by tragedy

Is redemption near can it ever be felt
When will I claim the victor's belt
"Fight on" is the cry scarcely heard
Combat, chaos, terrors, curse words

Cries for mercy go unattended
Surrender over death cannot be comprehended
Joyous spirit knows no quit
Life slowly drains from body's pit

Battle smoke clears but no end in sight
Wounded ego seeks to salvage birthright
Spirit gives chase now eager for victory
Habit soldiers protect their life history
Only to die by soul's relentless redemption
Life becomes love filled with intention
Holiness floats on the air in space
Victory is mine, Truth embraced.

Holy Lord, what is there besides love? What has substance without love? Can nothingness masquerade as something?

Turn my eyes to see only You. Have my heart live in the midst of Your love. Let me know with every breath that You are there.

Beloved One, this tinselled world glitters with useless baubles of temptation. My mind, my thoughts are drawn there. How limited is this pursuit, how valueless it's offering?

I pray that Your call is so piercing that nothing comes between You and me.

Make Your yearning the magnet that draws me to Your presence. Envelope me in a womb of love to be born anew in You.

Beloved Lord, how can I say that I have placed my mind in You when I have thoughts of judgement?

Can I say that I have surrendered to You when I uncaringly look upon my neighbour?

O, the hypocrisy of my attitude and the arrogance of its justification.

Blessed One, Your compassion knows only tender humility. Draw me close to its blessing that I might be close to You.

Open my heart to accept everything before me, with eyes focused only on You.

Can love recognize a boundary? Can joy be contained? Expand my consciousness, Beloved One, help me to break free from the confines of my limited mind.

Blessed Lord, when I say that I surrender to You, am I not surrendering that which is already Yours?

When I give my life into Your hands, is it not already there?

Take my love, Beloved One, for it comes from my yearning heart. Take it for it may be the only thing you cannot have unless I offer it.

Take it all, take every morsel. Accept it as a gesture of my devotion to You.

Guide me, Beloved One, to never hold back the choice of giving love to Your Holiness. Help me to never turn away from You through some self-centered judgement, some closed attitude.

Divine Lord, how do I abandon myself to your Love? How do I come to know that I am in You?

Giving my entire self to You is my only desire. Lead me, my Love—holding back for I know not what, is no longer an option.

My heart has surrendered, my will is dying. Only You, Beloved One, can save me.

I want You alone, without condition or reservation. The sight of You everywhere has turned my eye to the magnificent and my soul rests in the joy that its winter has passed.

O, tender Love of every moment. O, quiet joy of harmonious stillness. Wisps of light glimmering in the darkness—Thou art real.

All things are One. All thoughts are written on the divine scroll of infinity. All children love, some obvious and others disguised.

O, Beloved One, accept the changes in the ways I love You, that I might express personally that which You are for me.

My love is Yours, given by You and now returned with personality. Not to be better, for this cannot be, but as a variant for Your pleasure.

Divine Lord, is that the stillness of omnipresent joy I hear? The silent whispering of Love in my soul beckoning me to follow the light of heaven shining through?

With unheard footsteps and unseen hands, I am led to Thee.

O, Blessed One, how could I ever have doubted the sincerity of Thy covenant.

Tethered together, I ask that these eyes be deluded no more.

Thou and I are One.

Holy Lord, do I let You love me? Am I receptive to the fragile gestures of Your attention?

Do I allow myself to be caught in the consuming fire of Your yearning for me?

Is night different from day if the darkness is absent? Turn me to face You. Pay no heed to my cold indifference, to my distracted glances at Thy presence.

Lift me up, Beloved One, and open my eyes that I might be without You no more.

Your child can only grow through Your grace—feed me, Divine Mother, help me to consume Your love.

O, Beloved One, am I of gentle heart? Is it soft enough to feel for those who have lost all feeling, gentle enough to see Thee where others cannot?

Is my compassion great enough to be open to that which I do not understand, to hear that which I cannot fathom?

Help me, Holy Lord, to always stand in humility to accept all as coming from Thee. May I be humble enough to lose sight of myself and see only Thee.

Holy Lord, when I act do I do so in accordance with Your will?

In my behaviour do I represent You?

As I talk, is it Your truth of which I speak?

When I look out, is it You that I see before me?

Beloved God, help me so that no aspect of who I am might forsake You.

It is You that I want, You alone.

O, Divine Lord, is it You always looking at me with loving eyes?

Is it You looking into my eyes and me looking back at You?

Let me never stray from Your loving glance—from the look of affection that sustains the Love I feel.

In my love can I make amends for those who turn from You?

Can I transform the pain of the world through my gaze upon You?

Say it is so, Beloved Lord, that I might serve everyone in my heart and Your compassion may be made manifest in all my actions.

You are my Love and I surrender to You.

Divine Lord, I am aware of my intent to surrender all to You. How can I purify this, how can I realize this in every moment?

Lead me where I have not walked, reveal to me what I have not seen.

Fulfill the one desire of my heart—to live in You, breathe in You, love in You.

Help me, Beloved One, to become that which I Am.

Holy Lord, give me the strength to imitate Christ. That I might disregard all disappointments and ignore every ingratitude.

Help my head and heart to dwell in kindness, all the while knowing that it is You who stands before me.

Let me smile in the knowledge that as Christ suffered for me so I am able to accept the small disturbances of life, knowing that everything comes from You.

You are my Love in all things and I bow to You again and again.

O, my Lord, can I ever escape You? Can I ever hide from your omnipresent gaze?

I pray not, lest the warm breeze of Your love eludes me or the fragrance of Your joy is no more.

You are manifest in the souls around me and in the duty that lies before me.

It is in gratitude that I kneel before You. Grace sustains me and gives me life in You.

O, Lord, did You create me to make me happy through all eternity?

Was that the purpose of Your love for me?

This Love that is my breath, that is the blood running through my veins. This Love that nurtures and uplifts me when all else leaves me abandoned.

O, eternal Mother, may I rest my head on Your lap of omnipresence while You softly sing your lullaby of life to me.

I am Your child and You are the happiness that has become me.

Thank You, Blessed Love, thank You.

Beloved One, with all You have given me can I ever give too much?

Can those around me not expect that I see You in them and with Your grace, share with them all that has been given to me?

Can Your generosity be depleted? Can it be diminished or is it only through my own withholding that I cause its restriction?

Open me to see as You see, and with Your will of love, help me to serve all whom I meet as if I was meeting with You alone.

O, Holy Lord, in the cold morning air the warmth of Your love washes over me like a tide coming in.

And Your joy springs forth in my soul like the light awakening the dawn.

How do I come closer to You, Blessed One? Is it my pride that keeps me away? Is it the arrogance of my ways that blocks the way to you?

Help me, Holy God, that I might relinquish all that comes between us. May I sit at Your feet and forever be with You.

O, Divine Lord, may the gentle hand of Your love guide me through the forest of delusion.

Walk with me that I walk not alone. Talk with me that I might know of Your presence.

And as I stumble forgive me, for in my soul I want only You.

You who are the Light that shines before all things.

And even though my path is dark, through Your grace I am able to see my way to You.

Divine Lord, in the early light of dawn I catch wisps of Thy love floating like cottonwood blossoms on a zephyr of joy through the field of my mind.

Spring flowers line my path in a scent of anticipation wafting from a yearning heart. Love has become all that sustains me and my willing surrender is complete.

I take no thought of my next step. All that lies ahead is friendly for no harm can assail this fortress of bliss anchored to the ocean of Thy presence.

Peace has been made manifest and silence is the sound of love whispering through every atom of space, "Come to Me, Come to Me."

Holy Ocean of love, lapping at the shores of my soul. Light of eternal joy shining on the plain of my life.

Is it You who has led me to this place? Is it You that works in me—Doer of all things?

I am nothing but Your child waiting for You to enfold me in the petals of Your love.

O, Flower of my heart, accept the blossoms of my devotion that I lay on the altar of Your grace.

Accept me that I might forever be free in You.

O, Lord, is there ever loving too much? Can love become a burden when it is Your love flowing through my heart?

Lord, help me to love more, that I might be more open to welcoming the stranger while knowing in my soul it is You.

O the freedom of it, the sheer joy of living in a flood of love. It's a lake that has an eternal spring and all thrive who come to drink of its shinning water.

Teach me of Your ways, that I might imitate them and lighten the lives of those who are burdened.

Give to me that I may give to others. Open my heart in greeting to all hearts.

Long white yachts

Quiet peace of trickling mind tracks
Heartbeats thump in knowing climax
Joy's slow-moving eloquent eyes
Love knows there are no lies

Dawn awakens breaking day
Hope stands tall seeking new pathway
Light dissolves night's perilous fears
Hate jumps up to a chorus of cheers

Blackbird flies through clouds of grey
Spirit plods on with feet of clay
Thoughts erupt in an emotional fountain
Fingers cling to cold faced mountain

Elusive truth blind to sight
Will stressed searches what is right
Demented mind haunted playthings
Pieces of silver tied to life strings

Freedom facing unknown goal
Every sense demanding bankroll
Intuitive calling muddled in spots
Money answers in long white yachts

Desires evaporate on desert's mirage
Pain plays a tune—cardiac massage
Hopes abandoned holding the gun
Feelings, denial, senses undone

Where to now cry abandoned dreams
Heart explores high mountain ravines
Rains sweat on raw granite face
Path signs flash in memory trace

Walk isn't easy stinking and cursed
Silent will tramps on unrehearsed
Ego tantrums face down in the dirt
Route cut thin danger alert

Wandering attention windmill senses
Pieces of wisdom raise defenses
Gnawing doubt makes cheap talk
One raven jumps while others squawk

Breath's rhythm slows heart's furious beat
Settling thoughts debate indiscreet
Brain flashing stillness, moment of ease
Intuitive knowing admits ego's disease

Soul eye's highway made straight
Knowing truth's golden gate
Grace unbridled gallops ahead
Joy becomes bliss, love's arrowhead

Divinity looking front and back
Acceptance, freedom, joy's counterattack
Love without judgement, guilt undone
One shining light, a midnight sun.

Beloved God, with all I have in this world You are still my treasure. This gold and silver of Your love are all I need.

Divine Lord, You know the poverty of my heart. Come to me, that I might be fulfilled in You.

Capture me, that I might surrender the nothingness of myself to the majesty of Your omnipresence.

Leave no remnant of my desires behind, to tempt me to return to the delusion of my past without You.

Your child cries for You. Come, Beloved One, and wipe away the tears of ages that my soul may at last find You.

How can I resemble You, Lord?

What quality shall I take so that I may say I am like You?

Come closer, why are You so distant? Or is it me that holds You away in the activity of my importance?

Can we be of One Heart, with me beating, breathing and living in You?

You who are Love, I surrender to You that I might become that which You are.

May my love become Your love and may I through Your grace always live at Your feet.

O, Divine Lord, my soul doth rejoice in knowing that Thou art my God.

A joy springs up within me that captures my heart, the reward of which is untold by any lips.

As I rest in Grace beneath the wings of Thy protection, carry me higher, Beloved One, that I may see shores unseen and hear truths untold, according to Thy will.

The wildfire of my desire for Thee burns the dross of every limitation. I stand free, feeling the breath of Thy love surrounding me.

Tarry with me my Love, linger through all eternity.

Beloved God, the experience of Thy joy surpasses all earthly pleasures.

With Thy presence coursing through my veins, dawn has broken.

Thy child is awake to the guidance of Love.

Lead me beside still waters that I may rest beneath the boughs of Thy all protecting mantel.

My will is surrendered, it's function complete. I now walk only in Thee.

Holy Love, how could I ask for more and yet this is only the beginning.

Will my heart burst, will this ever end? The sunlit feeling of magical lightness coursing its way through my body like a streamlet bubbling to the ocean.

How can I love You more? Is my surrender sufficient? Every cell of my being bows down in gratitude to You and I present all I am as an instrument for Your service.

A crystal lake of undisturbed peace bathes me in iridescent bliss. I am baptized, arising anew in You and forever free.

Divine Lord, I have heard Thy whispers of love on the breeze. I have seen Thy joy in the blossoms of spring.

I have waited in the high mountains of devotion and sat on the shores of peace calling to Thee, "Come to me, come to me".

When will You come desire of all desires and awaken me?

Leave me not as the bubble being blown by the gales of life, make me the ocean.

Divine Mother, as the ever-living waters of Thy love flow through me and the soft light of joy accompanies me, help me to always walk in the footsteps of Thy will.

Draw me close, Beloved One, that I might live in Truth unencumbered by the delusion of my human condition.

My soul cries for Thee, knowing that Thou art the Way, the Truth and the Life.

Come, Holy Spirit, I that I may be free.

Divine Lord, my heart bows to Thee again and again captured by the joy of Thy presence. And my mind rests in the stillness of peace.

O, Beloved One, stay not just as my summer guest but take ownership of this house, living here through all seasons as I surrender everything to Thee.

Be Thou the light shining before me, guiding each footstep. Be Thou the will behind every thought.

I am Thy child born in Love, accept me O, Holy One.

Beloved Lord, are You impatient to have me? In Your humbleness have I made you wait?

Through my indifference did I reject all Your advances, my arrogant will only loving itself?

O, Beloved One, is not a faithful heart a joy to You? Does a yearning soul bring You happiness?

I have become Yours, my Love. My eyes look inward and all I see is You—peace has settled upon my heart.

The treasure I sought has been found. My way is clear and Truth has set me free.

The wait is over, I am in Love.

Holy Lord, to what end was I created? For what purpose do I live?

Are the breaths I take part of Your divine plan, or is it just air I draw in and breathe out?

The yearning of my soul tells me to love, when I grow weary it reminds me to love more deeply.

Could this be my purpose? Could Your loving will be the reason for my existence?

Say it is so, Beloved One, lest I believe I live only for myself. I who am nothing without You, I who have no substance other than that given by You.

I now know my purpose is Yours, for Your will is mine. This is the only way I can be free.

Divine Lord, does my joy praise You as the blossoms praise the spring?

Is my love generous as the rain is generous to the earth? Do I give love without judgement to all who surround me?

Does my love in some small way imitate Your divine love?

Beloved One, make each heartbeat a soulful melody of openness that includes each person I encounter and disregards none.

May the path of Your will flow through me to all whom I meet.

Silver leaves blowing on the boughs of love. Blossoms scattered in a carpet of devotion.

I am the sky, blue reaching to infinity with the thunderous sound of Thy silence echoing in every atom.

With creation orbiting in my soul and the shining light of Omnipresence illuminating my mind—all is well.

Freedom remains undefined on the open plane of thoughtlessness. Love dawns in the wakeful state of simplicity and truth becomes the essential perimeter of each thought.

Beloved One, my gypsy heart has found Thee. O, treasure of changelessness, I surrender to Thy light.

Take me to far shores of new adventure. I am free in this crystal moment, shackled to Love and welded to Joy, as I fly my leaf unattached.

Holy Lord, an ocean of joy laps at the shores of my heart.

Heeding soul cries, I follow Omnipresent footsteps through starry nights of bliss and illumined days.

Wandering through infinity with the scent of truth filled flowers blossoming in all space—I know I have found Thee.

Beloved One, with ego exposed and all secrets revealed I now know the freedom of living in Thee.

Divine Truth, hold me fast that I might never again slip from Thy sight.

Light of my heart, God of all things, it is You who walks with me on this wondrous journey of joy.

I pray I shall never walk beside You or think outside of You. Take me in. Let not a word pass these lips without being of You.

O, Beloved One, the sky cannot know nor the earth understand how my soul sings unendingly, "I love You. I love You. I love You."

Divine Lord, where am I that You are not? Where can I search and find You not?

You are the center of all that I know I am—all that I have ever been.

The river of my dreams flows through You. The sun of my existence shines from the light of Your omnipresence.

O, Beloved One, take me deeper. Forsake me not on this path to Your heart.

Let me know You more intimately, help me to cast aside all desires except my yearning for You.

My Love, peace has become me and I am satisfied.

O, adorable God, You have blessed me and I am grateful. Thank You.

Divine Mother, the song of my heart sings praises of love to Thee.

A spring of ever-living joy trickles from whispered lips. Every experience is filled with the lightness of being.

O, Beloved One, take my hand and guide me down the pathways of life.

Calm this restless mind with only one thought—"Thou and I are never apart."

Divine Lord, I am contained in the canopy of Thy peace.

Resting in the blue sky of bliss and sitting on mountain peaks of love.

Looking out I see Thee on the infinity of my soul.

There are no words to describe the joy I feel living in Thy presence.

O, Beloved One, when the winds of delusion begin to blow, hold my mind steady so that not a thought shall pass untouched by Thee.

Sanctify me, my Love, to serve Thee in every circumstance.

The pleasure of a summer breeze's love hangs as scented roses on the breath of my yearning.

A gurgling stream of joy waters all thoughts of my mind. Rare flowers of untold devotion smile silently at the desire of my longing.

Peace has become me and heaven is all around. Gratitude defines my demeanor as my soul rests in Thee.

Stay with me, Beloved One, help me never to stray from the gaze of Thy love.

Red tin hat

Snow packed peaks arrow the sky
Bald eagle circles haunting cry
Black bear walks sunlit valley
Ocean's inlet reveals blind alley

Starfish blue cling to the bottom
Leaves blow along a breeze of autumn
Reflected light gleaming and coy
Memories flood back when I was a boy

Long days lived under African sun
Everything remembered was overdone
Carcasses eaten charred with fire
Servants would cook, I would hire

Heart awake, present this time
Day has come, no dream of mine
Things seem clearer but hardly that
Reality worn like a red tin hat

Shaded eyes look upon things new
Life's a lot like a vegetarian stew
Consideration, sentiment, pondered thoughts
You get what you have by casting lots

People demonstrate what's not right
Some bring sticks to a party fight
Love's gone missing it's all a flirt
No one wins and everyone's hurt

Eyes upraised beyond the hills
Is there a pill to remove these ills
Mind floats on smooth black water
Thoughts flame up and talk like a lawyer

Is this goal what life's about
Soul cries "no" in treacherous shout
More or less has little meaning
Emotions bartered, instinct intervening

Will courageous tries again
Remnant thoughts still remain
What lies behind mind's gentle song
Heart held focused, silence prolonged

Eternal melody begins to play
Soul rejoices in ego's dismay
Vast forests of love chant to the sky
Feelings laundered, left to out dry

Path widens, way becomes clear
Soul sees light like a blinded deer
Inner rejoicing becomes a spring
Mind remains still without bickering

Holiness flows in where it's always been
Bliss becomes joy's vending machine
Truth solidifies foundation rock
Life jump-started, electric shock

Happiness fills each void and crack
Smiles appear for there is no lack
Truth's assured of what's to come
Om beats loudly on ear's bass drum.

Divine footsteps walk on cosmic sea
Holiness present in each sand flea
Wind of beauty swirls all around
Things unnoticed are suddenly found

Devoted heart expands in joy
Had this feeling when I played with toys
Laughter fills the body frame
All is different but it's just the same

Now I know what I always knew
Truth pursued has become my view
Others may wonder how this came
I can't tell because it's just a game

Things so serious ought not to be
Love's a koala sitting in a tree
Life is funny when you see it a lot
Time to let go, undo the knot.

Divine Lord, walking in the joy of Thy temple, whispers of love echoing everywhere.

The soft light of Thy presence illumining the altar of my heart.

O, Beloved One, my soul is at rest in Thy glimmering ocean of everlasting peace.

I am no more, just Thee my God, just Thee.

O, Divine Love, my heart soars in the knowledge that You are my God.

As I wade in the Ganges of Your love, each footstep guided by the joy of Your will.

O, Beloved One, never leave me, lest when darkness comes I stray from Your embrace.

Hold the candle of Your love high that I might always recognize You in all things.

Divine Lord, a river of love flows through my heart and the sky of my soul shines in joy.

Mountains bow in acknowledgement to Thee and the lion lies down with the lamb.

Beloved One, may I forever live in Thee with each thought grounded in Thy presence.

O, Holy Love, hear my prayer that Truth might become me.

Love steps walking in a temple of joy, heart alight and mind at rest.

Every atom bowing at the sacredness of Thy presence.

O, Beloved One, Thy child is free in Thee.

I take no thought of what lies ahead.

Thee and Thee alone art my daily bread.

O, Divine Lord, with a heart set on You and eyes focused on the horizon of my mind.

It is Your love that lights the darkness as I wander down the lanes of life. And Your joy that stands as a beacon in the night.

Beloved One, You have never forsaken me.

Help me never to lose sight of You and wander into the forest of delusion where You cannot be found.

O, Holy Lord, in the first glimmer of dawn the certainty of Thy love assures my every step.

A sparkle of holy light dances across the fringe of my mind and the hammock of my soul sways in the breeze of divine peace.

The smile of summer surrounds every thought imploring remembrance of Thee.

O, Beloved One, I thank Thee for days without nights and a life without end.

Thou and I, never apart.

Holy Lord, it is with gratitude in my heart that I look out on this life of mine, seeing everything of value that has been given by Thee.

O, Silent Gift, giver of earth and sky, Holy benefactor of forest and ocean.

Thou hast bid me walk in the midst of Thy generosity asking for nothing but a knowledge of Thee.

O, Beloved One, awaken these slumbering eyes to see Thee everywhere. Sharpen this dull mind that not a moment shall pass without an awareness of Thee.

Divine Lord, on the wandering path of my heart just behind the horizon of closed eyes. There You wait in a golden arch of omnipresence, aglow in the glorious light of pure divinity.

O, how my soul rejoices and joy rains down upon my life.

O, Pillar of Fire, light my darkness, lift the shroud of silence that I might forever walk in the footsteps of Your will.

Holy Lord, although I have no words to utter, will You still listen to the love in my heart?

When I think no thoughts of You, will You hold a memory of me?

Beloved One, so often I have nothing to say as I gaze upon You. Let this loving stillness be my prayer. Let this gesture made in love be the joy felt in silence.

Without words let my love speak. Accept it, Holy One, as my offering to Your Grace.

Divine Mother, what are the things I hold for myself? Those things that exclude You.

Are they my ideas, the people around me, my work? What keeps You away? What magnifies the distance between Your heart and mine?

My Beloved, why is it that I yearn for You, yet hold You away?

Show me, Mother, teach me that You and I can be One. Live through me by Your grace.

Show me, Mother, what You want me to be.

Divine Love, how can I believe more fully that I am a joy to You?

How can I yearn more deeply to please You?

Should I purify myself? Should I more quickly recognize the distancing effect of my daily desires?

Help me, Holy Love, to come closer, help me to follow the promptings of Your will. Help me to love You without constraint or condition.

Come, my Love, lift up your fallen child from the pit of indifference.

Divine Mother, if I have confidence in myself take it from me. If I believe in my own strength, weaken me.

Let everything come from you. Let me have no trust other than You.

I will lean on You. I will turn every thought and gesture towards You.

O, Beloved One, show me that all the questions that are important to me will be answered by You.

Help me to gaze continuously upon you and free my love to meet with Yours.

Divine Lord, Thou art my gentle companion whose loving kindness paves the rough roads of life.

A simple stream of love beckons all who thirst with parched lips of delusion.

O, Changeless One, lead me forward that no clouds shall shade my sight of Thee.

With my soul at peace and eyes beholding beauty, my heart knows I have found Thee.

Holy Lord, You have asked of me to receive from the openness of Your truth.

What have I done? Have I closed my eyes to Your gifts? Have I looked longingly at this tinselled world and ignored your offerings?

Forgive me, Beloved One, the cries of my heart have awoken me. Receive I will. Expand my consciousness to receive the magnitude of Your grace.

In complete surrender, I wait knowing that Your offering is all I need to receive.

Help me, Holy One, from the narrowness of my sight to the vastness of Your consciousness.

Holy Dawn of Love, filtering through the clouds of every heart, reigning in the life of each person.

Open my consciousness to accept Thee in all Thy forms. Let not the judgements of arrogance hide the glory of my inheritance.

Beloved One, within Thee I am free. Awaken my eye that does not blink so that I might never lose sight of Thee.

O, Love, walk before me that I might hold fast to Thy hand of eternal grace.

Tall cedars of the heart how high you grow in the forest of my soul.

Branches touching heaven and roots planted in the earth.

Divine Lord, I am Thy child and river flows through me. At my core lies a shining meadow of peace.

I am grateful for Thy guidance. Offering wildflowers of devotion and this prayer as my promise never to leave Thee.

Divine Lord, pictures of past memories of Your presence flash through my mind. Circumstances long forgotten but love ever present.

Was there a time when You were not with me? Or a time when no joy was offered as a gift?

O, Beloved One, it was I who rejected You through my pride, believing I walk this path alone.

Accept me now as I surrender all on the altar of Your heart. And guide me that I never lose sight of You.

Holy Father, the hurricane of Thy love blows on the shores of my soul.

Scattering all delusions in its wake that the seeds of Truth might be firmly established in the soil of my heart.

O, Beloved One, will the equanimity of Thy presence console me? All I hold dear is vanquished and now I cling only to Thee.

Rescue me, shelter me from the storm—let the flood of Thy love preserve me until I feel the rock of Truth supporting me.

Shimmering water

O Jesus will you wait for me
Will you stay with me and be my Love
as I walk through skies of blue
Will You be with me when cold gales blow
and days have no light
Will Your lantern shine upon my path
in the blackness of my night
Tall trees of my heart,
swaying in the west wind of Your love
O Jordan of shimmering water promised land divine
enter into me that I may be Thine
Be thou my strength, my stronghold of everlasting joy
that hides not when faced with fear deployed
Let me live in You, let me be Your love
No failure can betray Thy sword of light
no pain pass through Thy shield of joy
O, my love, You fought for me
and died a valiant death that I might see
And in Your whispered promise You said
"Be thou my Love and let me set you free"
O, Jesus, have I grasped the magnitude of your act
do I understand the consequence of this fact

Sleeping soul arise and wait no more
become the Truth that I adore
Waste not a moment of this life
stray not on paths filled with strife
Manifest Love, be thou great
pour wellbeing on every hate
And whisper in unending melody
that Thou and I will always be.

Divine Mother, in the blush of the early dawn my thoughts turn to Thee.

As the cool air of the morning sways to the melody of Your presence and all creation awakens.

I rest in a shimmering lake of peace, the loon cry of Thy voice echoes in my soul.

O, Beloved One, I rejoice at Thy beckoning and follow in the footsteps of Thy will. Reaching out I touch the hem of Thy robe to be forever healed to live in Thee.

Holy Lord, the compass of my soul points towards Thee and every desire of the heart yearns for Thy love.

As the winds blow and the rains fall, Thy presence stands like a rock and all within is calm. A smile of joy touches every thought and my way is happy.

O, Beloved One, there are no words left but "Thank You", as I now live in Thee.

O, Divine Lord, walking in the midst of Thy presence, warm wind at my back.

Wisdom floating in the air with blossoms scent. Truth proclaimed in the birdsong.

My heart sores to where no eagle has flown, resting on the craggy peaks of Thy love.

And there, in every crevice lies treasure, a golden glittering in the star of my mind.

O, Beloved One, let this light of love so shine before me that as I'm led further I may never be without Thee.

Divine Lord, as the day awaits the dawn and the earth celebrates the passing of night, so my soul rejoices in thirsting for Thee.

Spring of ever living joy, the ecstasy of being immersed in Thy love is the greatest of life's secret pleasures.

O, Beloved One, awaken the consciousness of Christ within me that I might ever be one with Thee and follow in the footsteps of Thy will.

Submerge me in the ocean of Thy heart.

Holy Love of my soul, how my heart soars at knowing You are my God.

As I walk in the Ganges of Your love, each footstep is guided by the joy of Your will.

O, Beloved One, never leave my side lest when darkness comes I stray from Your embrace.

Hold the candle of Your love high that I might always recognize You in all things.

O, Beloved Lord, the love of my heart is surrounded by the peace of Thy ever-new joy.

The treasure I have discovered has made me rich beyond limit.

The footsteps of infinity echo on the still lake of my mind and Thy word is upon my lips.

My God, my God, capture me that no remnant of my consciousness might remain as I live forever in Thee and Thy will is done through me.

Divine Lord, the sunlit pleasure of knowing that You are God fills the garden of my life constantly watered with devotion.

All leaves point to You and every flower smiles at Your presence.

O, Beloved One, You are the harvest and I am the labourer, strengthen me not to waste a moment as my soul reaps the bounty of Your love.

O, Divine Lord, does the simplicity of Your love lie in its acceptance?

Help me to accept all that comes from Your hand without judgement, knowing that You hold my wellbeing in the highest.

O, Beloved One, take my hand lest I become lost in the grandeur of my own perceptions.

Nurture me, lest I believe that my own actions sustain who I am.

Holy Lord, I see Thy joy in all creation and perceive the wonder of its design.

I humbly thank Thee for the time Thou hast given me to play my part. But all the while my soul exclaims in glee that it has never left Thee.

O, Beloved One, turn my senses ever inward so that no glorious image played on the screen of life will ever capture my attention from the bliss of Thy everlasting presence.

Divine Lord, from the moment of my birth you have taken my hand in Yours.

Every footstep You followed, watching and guarding me. Every utterance You listened, waiting for an indication of my return.

O, Beloved One, there are no words to describe the joy my soul feels at being born again in You.

It is no longer of this world but rests solely on the pillow of Your love.

I thank You. I am so grateful to you O, Divine Mother.

Beloved One, I know that You help me in every way. I know Your whisper and Your glance.

My heart jumps in recognition of Your Love. O, glorious God, can I ask for more?

Increase my yearning and desire for You. Grow it, Holy Love, so that sleep cannot touch my eyes, so that delusion cannot cloud my vision.

Help me to see only You—recognizing You in every face, in every place.

Reveal Yourself, come closer Blessed Love—Your child cries for You.

Divine Love, the faith I have in You is it solid? Is it enough for You to recognize Your child's love for You?

I pray that You deepen this yearning so that my hunger and thirst for You are never satisfied.

Help me, Beloved One, that in my pursuit of You I do not fail.

Come to me true Love, let no thought or word from my lips pass without being saturated in You.

Come to me, that I may live in oneness with You all the days of my life.

Dear Lord, can You find rest in my heart? Is my love sufficient to welcome You?

Can You stay in my stillness ever taking me deeper, searching for pearls of Truth?

Is Your home in the hearts of all who love You? Is there solace for You in the gentle murmurings of prayers dipped in devotion?

I pray, Beloved One, that You may rest in me as I continuously find my peace in You.

You are my Love and it is You alone I desire.

Divine Lord, Your love washes over the fields of my life. Eyes dance, dazzled at the sight of Your omnipresence.

Recognizing all is good, kindness sprouts a crop of wellbeing and life is simple.

O, how my life is filled with joy knowing that all to come is You.

Truth manifested becomes the way of the soul, rested in peace.

I am Your child and I love You.

Divine Lord, what I love, I love for myself. I take this love into me and frame that which I am around it.

How can I love You for Yourself? How can I see You without interpreting the benefit to myself?

O, the arrogance of this view and the limitation of its benefit.

Help me, Beloved One, lest in my selfishness I come to believe what I have is the truth—when I do not.

Let not the mirage of my senses delude my soul into thinking I have You when I don't.

Make my love for you a rock that will withstand all seasons, while the self melts away with the rain.

Divine Love, how might I contemplate You at every moment?

Imprint Your mind on mine so that every thought comes from You, every whisper an idea of Yours.

Take my life, lest I live it for myself in the wasteland of delusion.

Take my habits good and bad, lest by repetition I fall into the abyss of indifference.

Make my life Yours so that I know only You.

Divine One, do the clouds search for rain? Does the river hunt for water?

Do I seek You enough? Do I search and pursue You at every opportunity?

Take the sweet scent of my heart's flowers. Take anything You wish, but tell me that I can never lose You.

Let me feel Your joy and see Your light, that I may forever kneel at Your feet.

You are my God and my soul rejoices in this truth.

A new playground

Pink blossoms of spring their story sing
Dancing on wind's wild flapping wing
Birds excited dart and warble
Sea's rough and cormorants snorkel

Life lays out in a sunny stretch
Dogs on the beach, balls to fetch
Thoughts wonder if this is it
The world seems made of a Meccano kit

It fits together but rather lose
Some people use it as the poor excuse
Meaning's lost in all I buy
When's the time of my last good-bye

Heart seeks to score even more
Will it find something to adore
Eyes do wander all about
Something inside wants to shout

What's the meaning of it all
Please don't say to go to the mall
How do I dig below the surface
When all I see is life's circus

Truth where are you bashful and bold
Heart of mine wants in from the cold
Desires no longer tempting and fresh
Habits taste old and wizen the flesh

Egos bombastic loud and proud
A cumulus sickness affecting the crowd
Petals lay still while trodden by feet
Everything's brash and indiscreet

The sound of silence my soul longs to hear
Is the whisper of truth in my ear
Closed eyes, focused and still
Quieten the mind's revolving windmill

Peace flows over an iridescent pool
Joy rises as an illumined jewel
Heart awakens to this current of love
An olive branch carried in the beak of a dove

Satisfaction located the meaning is clear
Soul's fighting like a brave mutineer
Hard to starboard the course must change
Lookout, watch for a high mountain range
Live in the peaks with valleys far below
Breathing thin air and eating snow
It's a life of discipline, austere and stark
High above the treeline and meadowlark

It feels so good truth to know
Life appears normal there's little to show
Mind's doors are open wide
No secrets left, there's nothing to hide

Surrendering I kneel before Omnipresent feet
Devotional flowers offered in a heartbeat
The scent of bliss carries me higher
Joy sings its song, a celestial choir

With eyes anew looking into the blue
All thoughts now focus entirely on You
My soul at rest has finally found
A place to wander, a new playground.

O, Lord, what did You dream for me? What was the picture of my existence in Your omniscient mind?

Was it the gypsy that roams and roams but seldom finds? Was it the ruler who takes all but gives little?

Tell me, Holy Lord, am I what You imagined on the day of my creation? Am I walking in the steps You determined for me?

Come to me, Beloved One, for I desire the love of Your will—may I do it always.

Holy Lord, it is now obvious that I am nothing unless filled with You.

The hollow caldron of my person is useless until filled with Your truth.

The words I speak carry no consequence unless they are pronounced with Your will.

You are life and if life is separate from You it has no value. The currency of meaning is wisdom. No dream contains lasting substance.

Awaken me, Beloved One, that I may see only the everlasting reality of which I am one.

Change my consciousness that every delusional desire for happiness is vanquished in love for You.

Divine Lord, do Your gifts ever end? Is there a point where Your grace ceases and is no more?

How have I not thanked You in every moment for Your surprises of happiness?

O, Beloved One, forgive the self-love that blinds all coming from You.

Turn my eyes upward. Help me to see only Your loving-kindness. Guide me to be that which is Your will. Open me to live entirely in You.

O, Lord, as the ocean rests between its shores and the valley sleeps between its peaks, may I place my will in Yours. May I forget myself in Yourself.

Let Your joyous breeze carry me like a cottonwood blossom in the direction of Your choosing.

Let all thoughts of my life meander through You as I hold my raptured gaze on the magnificence of Your presence.

Accept me, my Love, that I may always be in You.

Divine Lord, strengthen me to always give You my will, whether it be on a dark night or sun-filled day.

It is the intimacy of Your love that forever draws me to Your heart.

Help me, Beloved One, to increase and perfect this bond. Let not weariness or bodily difficulties excuse me from Your bliss.

I am Yours, with no desire of having a moment of my own. My moments are irrelevant and mundane compared with the joy of this intimacy.

My Lord, do I reject the gifts from Your hand? In my selfishness do I hold You away arrogantly believing I can walk this path alone?

You who are my substance, forgive me for my ungratefulness, for my indifference.

I am enfolded in Your presence and there is nothing I need but You.

Accept me, Beloved One, that I may grow in You and manifest the remainder of my days through You.

Divine Lord, the light of Truth shines upon my soul. All streams of thought flow towards Thee.

Thy mantle of protection shields me from the storms of life as I walk this path of joy.

O, Beloved One, the dye is cast and my surrender sincere as I kneel at the feet of Omnipresence.

Thy prodigal child has returned. Accept me, Divine Lord, accept me.

Holy Lord, I find Thee in the mountains ahead and the lush valleys below.

Sacred air sustaining every breath. Soul singing in a garden of joy.

Dear One, I am at peace. Every person is my friend, yea even my enemies are cloaked in a face of Holiness.

Placing my unbridled gratitude on the altar of Thy heart, I pray for oneness with Thee leaving no remnant of self behind.

Accept me, Holy One, accept me.

Divine Lord, do I live for You or for myself? Do You come first, do I serve You before I serve myself?

O, the arrogance of my glib answers and tinselled platitudes.

Let me not delude myself, but kneel before You surrendering every thought and desire. Let each word passing my lips be filled with adoration for You my glorious God.

How can love grow if it is not reciprocated? When have You ever not loved me? When did You not serve me?

O, Beloved One, forgive my cold indifference. Forgive the thoughtlessness of my blind actions.

Through Your grace, I see the error of my ways and now pleasing You is my only desire.

Divine Lord, the love of my heart is surrounded by the peace of Thy joy.

Lo, the treasure I have discovered has made me rich beyond measure.

The sound of Thy footsteps echoes on the still lake of my mind and Thy word is upon my lips.

O, Beloved One, capture me that no remnant of my consciousness might remain as I live forever in Thee.

And Thy will is done through me.

Lord, is there an end to Your gifts? What do You not give?

Can my eye blink if it is not for You? Can a tear fall that You know not of?

O, how I have been blessed through Your gifts.

Divine Lord, I am Yours. Let the life You have given me be my gift to You.

Do with me what You will, all I can say is that I love You.

Divine Lord, increase my yearning for You. Have it encompass all the moments of my life.

Let it be the dawn that awakens me and the sunset of my sleep.

Let it be in the stranger as I welcome him and in my friend as I cherish her.

Holy One, I pray that this hunger may never cease—may my thirst for You never be quenched.

O, Spring of ever living water, become a blazing river of light shining in my consciousness and through my eyes to see only You.

Beloved Lord, I offer You all the flowers of my heart. Those rare blossoms grown in the high crags of devotion.

Will this gesture bring You forth? Will You reveal Yourself to me?

I have no more to offer. My love is my only store of wealth and I am rich beyond measure—all through Your grace.

Come to me, Divine One, it is You alone that I seek.

I wait for You as a bride waiting for her groom.

O, Holy Lord, set my soul ablaze with the fire of Your love. Open my eye of wisdom to see all that is You.

When cold winter winds lay waste all thoughts of hope, allow me to take refuge in the warmth of Your compassion.

Through Your grace may every frigid criticism and judgement melt.

Open wide the skies of my heart so every beat echoes Your name.

O, God of Love, come to me that I might forever be in Your peace.

Lord, is there anything I cannot be in You? Are You everything happening in my life?

Are You the silent sound of the zephyr wafting through the forest? Are You the caress of rain on my cheek?

What are You not, Beloved One? Is there any occurrence that You are not part of?

Is not all that comes to me, You—reminding me to return to You?

Accept me, Lord, I surrender to You.

Divine Lord, was it with intention You created me?

Help me that I might purify my intention to be one with You. Help me to cast all cares aside focusing only on Your omnipresence.

May I see my Self in You. May I melt into your loving heart and lose all I believe I own.

You are all I want, you are my only desire.

O, Lord, how many opportunities do I lose in not returning a smile for a scowl, acceptance for irritation?

How often do I look at those around me as separate from myself?

Is my disinterest in them a rejection of You—are You not also who they are?

Guide me, divine Lord, to hold You ever before me so that all I participate in, I see through the lens of Your love.

Slave taken hostage

Windswept cliffs echo ocean's roar
Gale cries, spume flies, albatross soar
Black rocks kneel devoted oblation
White waves crest standing ovation

Lightning flashes through canyon's arch
Hoping to know in processional march
Craggy rock walls hide unseen truth
Evidence hidden doubts uncouth

Naked mind of turbulent sea
Desires, habits, drenched sensuality
Waves bash crash, spray thinking
Pieces of silver bartered and tinkling

Clarity searches peaks of high places
Wisdom's hand opens infinite graces
Meadow flowers blossom in knowledge
Reason argues, slave taken hostage

Mind meets master, slowly tamed
Tested will cannot be shamed
Thoughts rebel with devious delight
One by one each surrenders the fight

Calm lake mirroring opalescent peace
Spirit's thoughts decoded with ease
Heaven's face rapt in humble respect
Creative love flows through depths unchecked

Happiness awaked, will compliant
Heart absorbed, spirit defiant
Oceans sway beneath sky's intention
Love found resting in focused attention.

Dear Lord, You have given to me from the time beyond memory.

How can I serve You now? Can I see through Your eyes where there is a need?

Can I set all petty judgements aside and give impartially?

Help me to open my heart that all who see it, see You.

You are my Love—just You. You alone.

Blessed Lord, You are the reason for my life. Thought of truth, source of all joy, happiness in communion.

Saturated with You, no appearance of separation, no gesture of rejection.

Is this enough, is this all? Oneness has become me and I am that.

Wind of eternal Love, sun of unfiltered delight can I please You? Can I offer You some small part of that which has so generously been given to me?

O, Beloved One, guide me ever inward to meet Your tenderness, to touch the eternal kindness.

Love can no longer be constrained—it is freed in the acceptance of Oneness. It is made real in the assurance of Faith.

Holy Lord, my mind is a bramble bush of crossing thoughts. I try to center it on You but mostly this desire is lost in idle uselessness.

Help me Lord, to strengthen my will, to place it unfailingly in Yours.

The fire of Your love is alight in my heart—I feel its warmth. I see the reflection of Your presence in its glow.

Stay with me Beloved One that the gravity of my humanity might dissipate to become a joyous celebration in You.

Divine Lord, the sun shines on my heart as I walk through the warm meadows of my life.

Picking the flowers of Thy blessings while resting beside the lake of everlasting Love.

Thou art my joy. Thou art all that I want.

O, Beloved One, lead me yet further that I may know Thee more intimately in all the days I have left.

Blessed Lord, with every action, help me to purify my motive. Let me see all that I do that is not for You.

Show me again, many times over that the "I" that I have cherished for so long is nothing.

Make the reality of that which I am apparent.

Reveal Thyself, Beloved One, that I may behold Thee and know from whence cometh my help.

Awaken me that I might sleep no more in delusion. My heart cries to know Thee. My eyes yearn to behold Thee.

O, Divine Lord, how great is Thy Love? Has it always been or is it new in each person?

How immense and intense is it? Does it occupy all space or is there a place where it is not?

Does my cold indifference diminish it? Does my ignorance diffuse it?

Beloved One, say it is not so. Whisper to me that Thy Love has never ceased and cannot be increased.

That is my prayer—that I am in Love always.

Holy Lord, how do I withhold from You? How do I keep for myself rather than giving to my Self?

Is there anything in me that is not of You?

Is not generosity giving all that I have been given? Is it not emptying the vessel that it may be filled anew?

Beloved One, help me to be Your generosity, Your love and Your goodness that I might be filled with You beyond measure.

Holy Lord, am I Your friend as I am Your child?

Do I invite You to laugh with me? Do I find joy in meeting with You although You are always with me?

Can I sit with You sharing both the relevant and unimportant times of my life?

Be with me, Beloved One. Every moment with You takes me higher, Best Friend.

Divine Lord, may I reverently make You an offering of my inadequacies that by Your grace they might be changed into something useful to You.

Are these not the cause of my suffering, is it not when I stumble and fall that I lose sight of You?

Help me to serve Your will, even in my smallness and especially when my strength abandons me.

Beloved One, I take no thought of my life without You—make what I have to Your liking.

O, Holy Lord, as I see the flowers of spring blossoming in my heart.

And the omnipresent green of the leaves all pointing to Thy love.

Looking down I see the petals of a perfect flower trampled beneath the feet of passers-by. Lo, Thou art there, hiding but still apparent.

Help me, Beloved One, to see Thee where I see Thee not, to love Thee where I love Thee not.

I pray that the spring of joy in my heart may ever bubble forth giving to all who drink, sight of Thee.

Dear Lord, how am I to become holy if it is not You who makes me so?

I know that holiness is not earned but given freely through Your grace.

Quieten my yearning heart and fill me with divine light.

Possess me that I might become a blossom scattered on Your altar of peace and let only Your will be done.

O, Lord, is Thy will nothing but love? Is it the gentle caress of Thy omnipresence in all things?

Can I accept this and surrender my heart unto Thee?

Enfold me, holy Beloved, that I might always be awake in Thee.

Thy love is the Ganges of my joy—never ceasing and ever new.

O, dawn of Tenderness, warm me with the glow of Thy glance and draw me onwards, always towards Thee.

Divine Lord, help me to go beyond the limits of my love.

Beyond the limits of my wanting to love and my surrender to love.

Help me to expand into Your omnipresent Oneness.

May I simplify each thought and action to include You, in both the relevant and irrelevant.

You are who I Am, how can I withhold from You?

Clarify my sight so that in faith I will always rest in You.

Divine Lord, Thy guiding hand reaches out and makes my crooked path straight—every obstacle replaced with love.

Through Thy grace, I have sandals for my feet and a coat to keep me warm.

O, Blessed One, make me worthy of Thy gifts. Help me to manifest Truth to all those around me according to Thy will.

Let not my mind wander to thoughts of my wellbeing but hold it firmly concentrated on Thee alone.

Holy Lord, as the day awaits the dawn and the earth celebrates the rain.

So my soul rejoices in yearning for Thee.

The simple pleasure of being immersed in Thy love is my desire of all desires.

O, Beloved One, awaken the consciousness of Christ within so I may forever be one with Thee.

And follow in the footsteps of Thy will.

Divine Mother, the simplicity of Your love shines on my heart like a light.

Peace comforts my soul.

As the mountains stand tall against the sky and forests move in the breeze.

So You walk with me and talk with me.

Beloved One, there is no more to ask for, there is no more to take.

You are my God and I live solely for Your sake.

Divine Lord, the soft rain of Thy love waters the garden of my heart.

The light of Thy omnipresence shines before my eyes.

It is in joy that I beckon to Thee to come closer.

O, Beloved One, let no storm divide us, let no thought or memory cause me to lose sight of Thee.

I am Thine and Thou art mine and that is the truth.

Messerschmitts

Cars ride through the humid night
One man argues and others fight
Motel room smells of sick
Is this road the one I'd pick

Every street looks the same
Some people walk but many are lame
Traffic's crazy and sometimes ferocious
People seem normal and others atrocious

The road I'm on has some scary bits
Keep a lookout for the Messerschmitts
Things blow up and dreams do die
Am I living the truth or a lie

With eyes cast down I try not to look
Does anyone here have a guidebook
Most of the time I've lost my way
All the while trying to avoid the fray

Take a left turn and look for the ocean
Try to escape the constant commotion
Long sandy beaches stretch for miles
Suddenly my heart bursts into smiles

Something within says I've left the din
Mind quiets down, meditation begins
Waves break on a peaceful shore
Joy enters through the open door

Pelicans surf the updraft wave
Fish dart out of an underwater cave
I'm swimming in light blind to sight
Ocean's roar is loud and filled with might

Thoughts hardly relevant, all eradicated
Silent words so long anticipated
Heart jumps at the sound of love
Soul knows what this's indicative of

Slowly the ego's will starts to melt
Feelings arise which are seldom felt
A sense of wellbeing breaks the surface
Life appears to have a purpose

Tears of rain fall on ocean below
Mind is a light reflecting rainbow
Things now seem to take their place
Life's no longer a hit in the face

The long road home has just begun
Stars, galaxies, beyond the sun
Oceans and islands whirling in space
Travelling to them by divine grace

Wave playing on the eternal sea
Now no bombers can get to me
Slowly developing from a long way out
Starting to crest—breaking out

Life's end will come without a glance
Soul's doing the jive and a belly dance
The transient form that rode the ocean
Melted to become one harmonic motion.

46182636R00089

Made in the USA
Middletown, DE
25 May 2019